THICH NHAT HANH

ANXIETY CONTROL IN 30 MINUTES
THE ART OF BEING IN PEACE

AARON ANDERSON

CONTENTS

CONCLUSION

CONGRATS! NOTE FROM AARON ANDERSON:

PREFACE

Anxiety disorders are one of the most common mental illnesses that we face today. In the US alone, over 40 million aged 18 and up experience some level of it every single year. But despite the amount of times anxiety is experienced through us, there are several ways to be treating anxiety. Some of these things can be a matter of staying active, avoiding alcohol or smoking, ditching caffeine, and opting for a healthy diet.

While these are life-changing habits that can transform your life, these are often things people will struggle to commit to. But one lifestyle change that many people find easier to grasp is meditation.

Meditation for anxiety is something that can be integrated easier into people's lives than they might think. You can meditate anywhere and at any time and it only takes up a handful of minutes in your long day. It feels easier to incorporate than quitting a bad habit, changing your entire diet, or squeezing in more time in your day to exercise.

That said, meditation comes with its own complex challenges that take a much different shape. Looking around the internet you'll find people struggling to "think" their way out of anxiety or use meditation to stop negative thoughts or to cure their anxiety through this method.

While these people all mean well, seeing meditation in that way is irrational. And that's not just me saying it. Vietnamese monk Thich Nhat Hanh believes the importance of meditation is around breathing.

It's setting aside what meditation could do for you and instead prioritizing the act of doing, practicing, and breathing.

He actually developed a light breathing exercise that you can incorporate into your daily life. This will lead you to a better experience with mediation and help you with feelings of anxiety.

MEDITATION

WHY IS THICH NHAT HANH BREATHING EXERCISE IMPORTANT?

"Breathing in, I calm body and mind. Breathing out, I smile. Dwelling in the present moment I know this is the only moment."

- Thich Nhat Hanh

Meditation is able to strike at the core of anxiety as many individuals claim. It makes sense since there are several studies that talk about meditation improving our mental state, or that it regulates our emotions.

Beyond that, anxiety is a mental illness so it's easy for people to see why meditation is something that can cure anxiety.

But true anxiety recovery is again more about doing, practicing, and breathing. It's more about you exercising your mind and learning how to interact with your emotions in a different way. You're focusing more on changing the links that are connected from your current mindset or thoughts to your body's responses to that mindset or thought.

As Thich Nhat Hanh says in his quote above, breathing in and out allows him to be in the present moment. This is vital for your anxiety recovery since you no doubt live in the past and regret your decisions many times. Those fearful projects then push you into the future where you aren't quite yourself.

Another way to look at this is that your anxiety - and worry - will push you to think about what "might" happen later down the road. And though all of our futures are a mystery, you shouldn't speculate much on what could happen in the future. What matters is where you are now and what you are currently doing.

THICH NHAT HANH'S SHORT BREATHING MEDITATION EXERCISE

Thich Nhat Hanh (Tick-Not-Hawn) developed a breathing exercise that's specifically designed for those who suffer from anxiety. It's been spread around the internet and many people are finding this method to be a great relief for them. It's got a simple and easy to memorize practice as well and best of all it only takes one minute to perform entirely.

That said, you can turn this into meditation practice for much longer if you feel it's appropriate. Meditation after all is one of those activities that you can take many liberties with. Below are the steps you need to complete:

- First, find a place to sit down comfortably. Afterward, close your eyes if you can and gently focus your attention on your breathing. You don't need to be concerned about deepening or controlling your breathing in any way. The focus is again on notice.
- As you are breathing in, say to yourself "I am breathing in." As you are breathing out, say to yourself, "I am breathing out."
- To keep this a short exercise, you'll be repeating the second step for a whole minute. Again, if you need to take longer than a minute, feel free to do so.
- The last thing to note is that the effects of this meditation are cumulative. The more often you practice this, the faster your overall level of calm will increase over time.

That's all there is to it. So the next time that you are ever feeling your anxiety kicking in, be sure to practice this. Even during times where you're not feeling anxiety, be sure to practice it. Out of the many meditations, breathing meditation exercises allow you to bring yourself to the present moment.

This is key as the present moment is where all of our solutions, happiness, and peace are found. It's the only place where our lives are all happening.

THICH NHAT HANH MEDITATION TECHNIQUES

But while the simple breathing meditation can help with your anxiety, there are several other alternatives. Maybe you'd prefer to have a longer meditation session and focusing on your breath isn't cutting it. Or maybe you'd like to try different techniques.

Thich Nhat Hanh has developed all kinds of different meditation techniques that help with anxiety. These particular techniques that are outlined below allow you to rewire your brain to be present with yourself.

This is essential as those who suffer from anxiety often dwell in the past and worry about the future rather than staying present. Some other techniques that he has instructed on include:

- Mindful breathing
- Concentration
- Awareness of your body
- Releasing tension
- And mindful walking

Here is a look into each technique.

Mindful Breathing

"From time to time, to remind ourselves to relax and be peaceful, we may wish to set aside some time for a retreat, a day of mindfulness, when we can walk slowly, smile, drink tea with a friend, enjoy being together as if we are the happiest people on Earth."

- Thich Nhat Hanh

One of the reasons the simple breathing exercise works is that we are always breathing. The same logic holds true with this technique and has many similarities to the simple version. Your goal is to pay attention to your breath as you would normally, but Thich Nhat Hanh takes a different approach than the exercise above.

While in the exercise you are to be breathing in and out while with mindful breathing, you're paying attention to everything. From whenever you breathe in and out to the length of each breath too.

As Thich Nhat Hanh explains:

"Please, when you breathe in, do not make an effort of breathing in. You just allow yourself to breathe in. Even if you don't breathe in it will breathe in by itself. So don't say, "My breath, come so that I tell you how to do it." Don't try to force anything, don't try to intervene, just allow the breathing in to take place...

What you have to do is be aware of the fact that breathing in is taking place. And you have more chances to enjoy your in-breath. Don't struggle with your breath, that is what I recommend. Realize that your in-breath is a wonder. When someone is dead, no matter what we do, the person will not breathe in again. So we are breathing in, that is a wonderful thing....

From those instructions, you can tell already it's getting you to look at your breathing presently and in deeper detail. Your breath is calming, but also keeps things real. The beauty of this technique is that it allows you to breathe naturally - based on your current emotions. It doesn't force you to breathe slowly or for long periods of time. This fact alone makes it easier for this technique to be adopted into your life.

Concentration

"Anxiety, the illness of our time, comes primarily from our inability to dwell in the present moment."

- Thich Nhat Hanh

To Thich Nhat Hanh, concentration is one of the seven factors of awakening and is, therefore, a great source of awareness and happiness in our lives. Concentration means being able to focus on something, though in meditation it means something simpler. Your breath, a flower, a spot on the wall, a body part. The idea is to direct your focus - for the moment - on something while practicing mindfulness.

To really make this meditation work, it's suggested that you choose something where you don't need to scan your eyes or anything. Buddhist monks often use a candle flame to focus on. Even if you get distracted by your thoughts, it's as simple as focusing back on the object.

For those starting out, maintaining concentration for long periods of time will be difficult. Even if you think you're an exception, society has been primed to be distracted by outside things. Social media, video games, food cravings, and more have all primed us to be dopamine addicts - that joy from doing something and giving ourselves that pat on the back sort of feeling.

A good start with this technique is to spend a minute on this technique and continue to increase the time every day.

If you're not sold on this technique, Thich Nhat Hanh explains the importance of this technique and why it's so powerful for us to be using it:

"Anything can be the object of your meditation, and with the powerful energy of concentration, you can make a breakthrough and develop insight. It's like a magnifying glass concentrating the light of the sun. If you put the point of concentrated light on a piece of paper, it will burn. Similarly, when your mindfulness and concentration are powerful, your insight will liberate you from fear, anger, and despair, and bring you true joy, true peace, and true happiness."

Awareness of Your Body

Not every breathing or concentration technique will work wonders for you. In some cases, those who suffer from anxiety might benefit from touch techniques. This particular technique is one that Thich Nhat Hanh suggests using if you are looking for more body awareness.

All that this technique involves is a body scan where you'll be focusing on each part of your body individually. While going through each segment of your body, you want to release any tension you're feeling and to relax.

This technique is great as we rarely experience this in our day to day lives. We see our body and it moves, but we're so distracted or thinking about other things that prevent us from living in the moment.

Thich Nhat Hanh suggests using the mantra "Breathing in, I'm aware of my body." This particular mantra compliments the mindfulness breathing technique mentioned above as it brings awareness and improved in and out-breath. You'll also find that using both of these techniques together will make it more peaceful and harmonious. If you continue to practice it that way you'll get a better feel for your body which will only help you further.

Release Tension

The fourth technique is to release tension. This meditation technique builds on the awareness of your body as you'll have to focus on tension around your body of course. Once you have more body awareness, you'll be able to release that tension from your body.

How you can do that is simple as Thich Nhat Hanh explains:

> *"So next time you're stopped at a red light, you might like to sit back and practice the fourth exercise: "Breathing in, I'm aware of my body. Breathing out, I release the tension in my body." Peace is possible at that moment, and it can be practiced many times a day—in the workplace, while you are driving, while you are cooking, while you are doing the dishes, while you are watering the vegetable garden. It is always possible to practice releasing the tension in yourself."*

The more awareness of your body you have, the more you realize how tense you can get over the course of the day doing regular activities. This of course feeds into the other techniques mentioned so far, making the techniques easier and easier to perform and get into a routine of doing.

Mindful Walking

The final meditation technique that Thich Nhat Hanh adopted is mindful walking. Similar to mindful breathing, you let your breath take place without any effort. You're simply enjoying it. This same principle holds true in the case of this exercise. Your focus is to walk and enjoy it.

Thich Nhat Hanh explains this process nicely as well:

"You don't have to make any effort during walking meditation, because it is enjoyable. You are there, body and mind together. You are fully alive, fully present in the here and the now. With every step, you touch the wonders of life that are in you and around you. When you walk like that, every step brings healing. Every step brings peace and joy because every step is a miracle.

The real miracle is not to fly or walk on fire. The real miracle is to walk on the Earth, and you can perform that miracle at any time."

This type of meditation is proof that there is no universal form of meditation nor does meditation have to be something while sitting still. It can be enjoyed with plenty of relaxed movement too.

HANDLING NEGATIVITY

"To take good care of ourselves, we must go back and take care of the wounded child inside of us. You have to practice going back to your wounded child every day. You have to embrace him or her tenderly, like a big brother or a big sister. You have to talk to him, talk to her. And you can write a letter to the Little child in you, of two or three pages, so that you recognize his or her presence, and will do everything you can to heal his or her wounds."

- Thich Nhat Hanh

According to multiple theories of cognitive therapy, who you think you are, and how much you value yourself will determine how you view yourself as well as the world around you. Because of this knowledge, it's quite clear how negativity can have an impact on you. In fact, there is research that shows just how much pessimism can impact your feelings, emotions and overall mental health. These particular issues can lead to you feeling anxious and developing anxiety disorders from it.

Indeed, negative emotions have an affecting - if not controlling - aspect to our lives that make it difficult to escape its influences. Feelings of worry and anger can grip us in powerful ways and steer our lives. But the beauty about those emotions is that they can be controlled. This report will be going into more detail about those two aspects soon, but for now, let's focus on handling negativity overall.

After all, we don't just experience anger, worry, or other negative emotions spontaneously. There is an underlying problem or even belief that could be impacting you. Being able to look at negativity on a broad surface can help you with handling negativity overall.

HOW ASPECTS OF NEGATIVITY CAN IMPACT YOUR ANXIETY

In order to know how negativity is impacting you, you need to know what sort of negativity is out there in the world. Negativity comes primarily from two things: negative thinking patterns you're putting yourself through as well as what you believe in. It's important to make these two distinctions in order to know how each one is impacting you and how you can overcome them.

Let's go into detail about each one.

Self-Defeating Beliefs

> *"To be beautiful means to be yourself. You don't need to be accepted by others. You need to accept yourself."*
>
> *- Thich Nhat Hanh*

What you believe in - or your overall belief system - consists of three things: your personal views, attitudes, and values. Your beliefs will be with you wherever you go and will shape the way that you see yourself and the world around you. This is so important as no doubt those who are suffering from anxiety are experiencing some level of self-doubt or even self-defeating beliefs. This is dangerous as those thoughts set you up for failure and dissatisfaction in your life.

We see this time and again in so many ways. A prime example is social media. So many people are addicted to it because they are obsessed with notifications. By that extension, they also care about comments, likes, and shares of the content they're posting online. This level of obsession can become so toxic that people believe their own self-worth is determined solely by the statistics of their posts.

This sort of belief can also be based on accomplishments they've achieved, whether that's in big goals achieved or advances in career.

Imagine the shock of those people if they believe that and they weren't granted what they expected. A post getting fewer and fewer views or hate comments. A big failure in the goals that they wanted to achieve. A failed opportunity to get a promotion. As soon as they meet failure, those people can begin to doubt everything that they've set out to do. Their entire identity shattered.

When it comes to these kinds of beliefs, they can be broken into two categories: intrapersonal beliefs and interpersonal beliefs.

Intrapersonal beliefs are the beliefs that you have about yourself. In the case of self-defeating beliefs, these can be things like the belief that everything has to be perfect. Or maybe that you only do things based on the approval of other people or that your entire worth is based on your own achievements and success.

Intrapersonal is all about your views of the relationships that you have in your life. When adding self-defeating layers to it you could hamper your relationship by shifting blame onto others or taking the blame when it's not your fault. Other examples are a sense of submissiveness to yourself or that you do your best to avoid conflict out of sheer fear of it.

In either of these categories, the self-defeating belief system doesn't help you and it makes matters worse in your life. These sources can also manifest in anxiety in extreme cases. Fear of conflict can lead to you feeling worried about the course of a relationship or fear of cutting the relationship off. You can also develop anxiety in the case where you're experiencing failure from trying something different. You can have anxiety in those cases if you try again and you're bringing yourself into a scenario that feels similar.

Negative Thinking Patterns

"When you say something really unkind, when you do something in retaliation your anger increases. You make the other person suffer, and he will try hard to say or to do something back to get relief from his suffering. That is how conflict escalates."

- Thich Nhat Hanh

The second category is negative thinking patterns. These are different from the self-defeating beliefs as negative thinking patterns aren't always stemming from you. Instead, these tend to emerge when you are faced with a problem. These are also called cognitive distortions and emerge during times where you are stressed out or feeling stuck. These reinforce those self-defeating beliefs and cause you to crack and break down.

An example of this is to say that your self-belief is that you value yourself based on your past achievements. While you will feel okay for the time being - especially when you are consistently reaching your goals - it's difficult to predict that your state of mind will always be like that. Life happens and there are times where you are faced with setbacks that you couldn't have prevented. In some cases, these can cause you to fail your goals utterly.

It's in these scenarios where negative thinking patterns thrive as they can cause you to over-analyze or exaggerate the severity of a problem. This can lead to triggering anxiety within yourself.

You'll start to believe yourself as a failure or you'll start blaming those around you or other circumstances for why you didn't succeed. In certain cases, you can start to think that you'll "never be a success" or that "it must not have meant to be." Thoughts like these will continue to persist and impact you in so many ways, leading you to avoid certain things, lowering your self-esteem, and could even lead you to depression.

Overcoming These Negative Emotions

"People have a hard time letting go of their suffering. Out of a fear of the unknown, they prefer suffering that is familiar."

- Thich Nhat Hanh

Overcoming these two aspects is difficult but not an impossible task. First of all, personal beliefs are something that we are taught and have developed over time. While these are difficult to change - especially when reinforced constantly - they can change through continuous practice.

It's for this reason the several meditation techniques mentioned here also have mantras tied to them in some capacity. These mantras instill a belief that allows you to make those shifts little by little.

Much like techniques for managing anger that is mentioned below, it's key that you address these issues and acknowledge them. Many people choose to bottle up these issues and that in turn influences their views and reactions to problems and the world around them. If you don't address these problems, you'll never be able to face them or begin to heal and grow from them.

Once that is complete, the next step is being able to challenge them. For example, if you feel inadequate about yourself, question whether that is true that people only accept you free of flaws or imperfections. Do you really think you're a loser or a failure if you don't obtain a level of success? Even after making numerous successes in the past? A failure is someone who fails to gain anything from any endeavor and there is always something good to be gained from any experience - be it a good experience or a bad one.

The idea is to continue to dispute those thoughts and beliefs, slowly replacing these with positive but also realistic ones. The more you challenge these the more you start to notice how those previous thoughts are not true at all.

Whenever you are faced with negativity, try some of the meditation techniques mentioned here and use them as opportunities to combat negativity.

HANDLING ANGER

"Anger is like a howling baby, suffering and crying. The baby needs his mother to embrace him. You are the mother for your baby, your anger. The moment you begin to practice breathing mindfully in and out, you have the energy of a mother, to cradle and embrace the baby. Just embracing your anger, just breathing in and breathing out, that is good enough. The baby will feel relief right away."

- Thich Nhat Hanh

As mentioned, anger is one of the two common emotions that can stem from negativity. However, anger can also lead to feelings of anxiety too. To understand this connection, it's best to explain anger and anxiety in more detail.

Anger is easy to define emotion at first. We think of it as someone being mad or feeling antagonistic towards a particular person. It's a burst of negative emotion that is taught to us from an early age. This is what we believe in

But anger is more than that. First, it's not always a negative emotion. Instead, anger is more like letting us know that we've been mistreated or hurt. It informs us that someone is doing something that we don't like and that we need to do something about it.

Anger is still destructive, but it can also be understood and used as a tool for you to steer your life.

Anxiety on the other hand is us being fearful or uncertain about something. Similar to anger, this is something we're taught but it's not the whole truth. Anxiety can create excessive fear, worry, nervousness, and even apprehension over what could happen in the future. It's the cause of panic attacks and can be destructive as well.

But beyond these descriptions of what these two are, the two of them together have various interactions. The main interaction is that one can effortlessly cause the other to trigger.

For example, while you feel anxiety, it could be that you're angry about something. Having an outburst of anger can make it embarrassing and lead to people feeling anxious or nervous over what others will think of them now.

On the flip side, anxiety can also cause anger. If you feel like you're not in control, which anxiety does certainly cause, you could feel irritated or frightened about it. When this happens, you could gravitate towards anger. It could be subtle at first but it can grow more and more extreme given the chance.

Considering the relationship between anger and anxiety, you can find peace with your anxiety by learning to manage and nurture your anger into something good.

THICH NHAT HANH'S ANGER MANAGEMENT

"With compassion you can die for other people, like the mother who can die for her child. You have the courage to say it because you are not afraid of losing anything, because you know that understanding and love is the foundation of happiness. But if you have fear of losing your status, your position, you will not have the courage to do it."

- Thich Nhat Hanh

Managing anger is not an easy task as many people can tell you. Anger is like a raging bull, it won't easily stop when you tell it to stop and it can be very destructive. But the main focus isn't so much to make it stop but rather learn how to use that anger for something more productive.

According to Thich Nhat Hanh, anger isn't just something you have to manage. Instead, it's something that you have to take the time to understand. It's best described by two simple sentences:

"Peace work is anger work. Anger work is peace work."

What they mean by that is that in order to understand anger, we're actually making peace work - learning to be more at peace with ourselves and to control our emotions better. Over time, it could be entirely possible to approach a hostile situation and be able to talk and react to it in a peaceful manner.

But before getting to that point, the foundation encourages that we engage in the mud that is anger. We should allow ourselves to feel fully human. That we are fallible and that we are capable of making mistakes and delve into negative afflictions. Part of using our anger stems from acknowledging that our anger can be used in practice as a source of loving-kindness for not just ourselves, but those around us. And once you acknowledge that anger inside you you can start to have peace with various parts of yourself that make you uncomfortable or uneasy.

Even if your anger isn't the source of your anxiety, it doesn't mean that you never get angry. There are things that you have no doubt buried that you're not proud about. Even if you feel like they are gone, you could still be struggling with them inside of your head. Even so, there is no doubt that you know someone in your life right now that does have anger issues as well.

From this point, the Thich Nhat Hanh Foundation provides three steps for you to help in understanding anger and having stronger control over it.

First, Acknowledge Your Anger

"Anger is just an emotion."

- Thich Nhat Hanh

This report has already mentioned this, but it's worth going into further detail about this point. The point of acknowledging anger is that it allows you to become more whole. Being aware that your anger is real is important as leaving it unattended can cause harmful effects. Even if you don't see it now, things like anxiety and anger can cause strains on the relationships that you have in your life.

Furthermore, it can cause conflicts that could have easily been prevented if you took better care of your anger or acknowledged other people's anger.

Part of the process is acknowledging, but also knowing more about anger. Anger is a force to be reckoned with, but since it's an emotion, it does have a place within us. It's merely an emotion that you are able to control. Not to control it in such a way you are denying the emotion or neglecting it, but rather working a loving relationship with anger.

Gain A Deeper Level of Understanding of Anger

There is much to anger but one thing is certain - it's important that you respect anger greatly. Again, controlling anger isn't an easy thing to do. It can take time to get back to a place of peace, clarity, stillness, and loving-kindness. When you touch someone else's anger, you'll have to deal with the karma of that. On top of that anger is an emotion that can affect an environment in a very negative way.

No one wants to deal with it so it makes sense why many step back from it or repress the emotion. No one wishes to confront anyone's anger, even their own.

With that in mind, coming in with a place of respect for not just anger but all of our emotions can provide us with a deeper understanding of everything about ourselves. Anger can oddly be a gateway to answering several deep personal questions about ourselves. What is the source of what we value most in our lives? What are the things that we hold great value, to begin with? What are your fears and worries?

The various emotions that comprise ourselves can provide answers that allow us to have a deeper understanding of ourselves.

Define Anger

"I would not look upon anger as something foreign to me that I have to fight… I have to deal with my anger with care, with love, with tenderness, with nonviolence."

- Thich Nhat Hanh

The final step is to define your anger. While there is an apt definition of anger above, there are many ways to describe anger - especially in the context of this newfound relationship that you'll be working towards.

In a fashion, anger could be best described as someone we have to respect but also as a protector. It may seem odd but think about it in this way: have you ever had a callous before?

Callous is your body's reaction to how it deals with pain and sensitivities. For example, do you lift heavy weights or play any kind of string instrument? If you do, you'll notice callous building up in particular parts. If you're lifting weights, the callous will be at the base of your fingers, near the palm. If you're playing guitar, you can develop callous over the fingers you use to play the guitar.

Callous is there to protect those sensitive areas so that the next time you do those activities, it's not as painful. It's an extra layer of resilient skin.

Anger works in the same way. When you are sensitive, anger is usually underneath all of that and is being built up. When something sensitive is brought up, anger will come up and defend yourself.

The same can be said about particular actions. For example, people overdosing have more things going on than what people initially think. We don't always understand that people's desire to overdose comes from a place of wanting to block the pain. Maybe not to the point of committing suicide at first, but finding some kind of relief in those cases can lead people to that if that's their only option.

You can also extend that to harmful addictions as well. People are addicted to certain things because this is the only method they know of that can give them the satisfaction they crave deep down.

In those situations, those individuals are denying what they truly need for whatever reason. Anger is not so different from that as it always is hiding something sensitive that we wish to not bring to the surface.

THICH NHAT HANH'S STEPS OF MINDFULNESS

While the method above is a good way of controlling your anger, Thich Nhat Hanh also has some guiding steps to managing anger. These steps of mindfulness stem from what's mentioned above so it's worth putting this into practice.

Mindfulness of The Emotion

The first step is having mindfulness of the emotion. Again, acknowledging your anger is part of the process of using, appreciating, and accepting anger. Thich Nhat Hanh has two mantras that you can use while doing a simple breathing exercise. Choose whichever suits you best:

- Breathing in, I know that anger is in me. Breathing out, I know that I am my anger."
- Breathing in, I know that anger is in me. Breathing out, I know that I must put all my energy into caring for my anger."

This begins to set the stage for the next steps of using your anger. These mantras help as they instill in us 6 key aspects of anger. Anger is:

- Something that we are.
- Something that we should never judge or repress
- Something that allows us to focus on ourselves, never on other people.
- Something that prompts us to show care for, like an older sister caring for the younger sister.
- Something that prompts us to have insight, like a gardener seeing the beauty of compost.
- Something that'll gradually transform into peace, love, and understanding.

Cooling Down

From that state of mind, you'll be able to begin the cooling down process. Based on the principles, it's not about repressing but caring. How you can go about that is through four methods:

- Walking outside and practicing meditation,
- Moving from a point of understanding to compassion

- Gaining further knowledge of the roots of anger
- Becoming free of knots within ourselves.

Walking Outside

While walking outside, there are several mantras that you can perform. Going through all of them can also prove beneficial for you in managing your anger. The sequence goes as follows:

- Breathing in, I know that anger is here.
- Breathing out, I know that the anger is me.
- Breathing in, I know that anger is unpleasant.
- Breathing out, I know this feeling will pass.
- Breathing in, I am calm.
- Breathing out, I am strong enough to take care of this anger.

This practice further drives home the ability to acknowledge anger and train to shift your mindset little by little. It can rewire your brain to see anger as something that you can nurture and address in a calm and loving manner. Furthermore, walking around in a calming environment will further enhance this and benefit you as opposed to pacing in a spot in your home.

Moving from Understanding Anger to Showing Compassion

For anger to be nurtured, one must come from a place of kindness and love. Anger's source can stem from all kinds of things though it isn't always clear at first. Other emotions can cloud our judgment of what it might be. But when you are calm and are ready to understand, you can find the root causes.

These root causes can be:

- **Misunderstandings:** While these happen all the time in life, anger can stem from us not fully understanding someone's situation and we're jumping to conclusions.
- **Clumsiness:** You made a mistake that upon reflecting didn't make any sense. You could get angry because you are frustrated about your decisions at that time.
- **Injustice:** Your source of justice being tarnished by someone's actions. Whether you are closely related to that person or you're a bystander, you can get angry over the actions people are doing that don't agree with what you believe in.
- **Resentment:** Envious of someone else's success or overall position in life, regardless of if it's a reality or not.
- **Conditioning:** The environment that you dwell in conditions you to behave in a particular fashion. The environment could be where you spend most of your time as well as the people that you are around the most.

Understanding these root causes will help you pinpoint exactly where your anger is coming from. In this method, you want to take about a half-hour to be mindful of your anger and to see what the source is. This will give you time to transform your anger into something completely different.

Seeing and understanding are the elements of liberation that bring about love and compassion in your life. This method works wonders with other calming practices for this reason.

Gaining More Knowledge of The Roots of Anger

The third method is diving deeper into the roots. These go beyond the resentment, misunderstanding, clumsiness, injustice, and conditioning roots above. This dives deeper into two roots: primary and secondary.

The primary roots are focused on specific emotions around ourselves. The primary root can be a lack of understanding of what causes you to feel angry. It can also stem from your desires, pride, mere agitation, or suspicion of something as well.

Those primary roots then feed into the secondary roots. Those particular roots are the aspects mentioned above. They are the end results based on the emotions that you experience as the primary root.

How this all helps you is by knowing what other emotions you are experiencing, you are able to respond with help or through discipline from a place of compassion, now that you have understanding.

Being Free of Knots

The final process of being mindful of your emotions is becoming free of your knots. Knots in this case are like tense areas of ourselves. They have to be things that you are aware of and that you want to handle as promptly and as easily as possible.

Up to this point, this shouldn't be as much of a problem as the way to address a lot of these knots or problematic reactions is to let the past experiences come to a sense of mindfulness and understanding. Once you do that, you can begin to show compassion and love.

How you can do that is by breathing and smiling. You'll want to look at your various emotions without turning a blind eye to them and see them as byproducts based on the experiences that you've had in the past.

HANDLING WORRY

Similar to anger, worry is the other emotion that stems from negativity and has a close relationship to anxiety. With your mind in the past, you can begin to worry about situations that might not come to pass at all. Similar to anger - or any negative emotion - Thich Nhat Hanh has a simple method to help with overcoming these. Below is a brief description of each step.

ACKNOWLEDGING

Like with anger, the first step comes in acknowledging and recognizing the emotions. The path to long-term healing can't begin until you take the small steps towards positive change. This is not easy as negativity will always follow you and can pull you back.

But this becomes more tolerable when you anticipate this to happen and recognize your emotions.

CONFRONTING

Once you accept the emotions, you'll need to face it directly. Dealing with worry can be frightening at first. You have an instinctual feeling to suppress negative emotions or to lessen the damage through other means. While they seem comforting at first, these are destructive and useless to you long term.

You'll need to face your worries, fears, and anxieties eventually. One way to overcome that is through the meditation techniques mentioned previously and realizing that this is only a feeling.

GET COMFORTABLE

Once the feelings are merged, it's up to you to be comfortable with the feelings. Don't let resistance take over and break the path to healing. During this stage, it's ideal to practice mindful breathing or meditation overall.

The beauty of this technique is that it encourages you to pay more attention to your body. Whether it's tension in your body or an ache in your heart, paying attention to these is key. After that, it's a matter of calming those areas with awareness and gentleness.

LETTING IT GO

The fourth step is about letting go. However, actually letting go isn't as straightforward as it seems. This is actually the hardest step since it forces you to practice meditation. Letting emotions go as part of meditation is key but not something people can do with little or no experience in meditation.

But for those who know how to meditate, the idea of releasing emotions is letting the emotion come into your life willingly. You want to have clear sight and understanding and even compassion for yourself and this feeling.

Only after this can you get into the final step.

DISCOVERY

The final step is discovery. Discovery of the source of that emotion. Negative emotions can spring up for all kinds of reasons and manifest into worry or anger or fear or other emotions. Once you set aside the emotion, you'll have nothing but the root of those negative feelings and unhappiness. This can take shape in the perception or beliefs that you hold.

As you are discovering more about it, it pays to ask yourself why you are holding yourself to those kinds of thoughts. Do you truly need to control every aspect of yourself?

The answer to that question will eventually reveal itself once you are prepared for it.

CONCLUSION

Anxiety is a complex emotion that can spark all kinds of emotions in us. Thankfully there are several types of techniques out there capable of combating the various emotions through understanding, caring, and compassion for it.

Even if those emotions are all painful to experience, these are seeds that we have planted ourselves. It is up to us whether we choose to nurture them like devoted gardeners or neglect them.

And thanks to Thich Nhat Hanh's understanding and teachings, you can become a devoted gardener and grow your mind to new heights.

"Smile, breathe, and go slowly."
-Thich Nhat Hanh